THE PARADOXES OF MOURNING

ALSO BY DR. ALAN WOLFELT

Healing Your Grieving Heart:
100 Practical Ideas

Loving from the Outside In, Mourning from the Inside Out

The Journey Through Grief:
Reflections on Healing

The Mourner's Book of Hope: 30 Days of Inspiration

Understanding Your Grief:
Ten Essential Touchstones for Finding Hope
and Healing Your Heart

Companion Press is dedicated to the education and support of both the bereaved and bereavement caregivers. We believe that those who companion the bereaved by walking with them as they journey in grief have a wondrous opportunity: to help others embrace and grow through grief—and to lead fuller, more deeply-lived lives themselves because of this important ministry.

For a complete catalog and ordering information, write, call, or visit:

Companion Press
The Center for Loss and Life Transition
3735 Broken Bow Road, Fort Collins, CO 80526
(970) 226-6050
www.centerforloss.com

THE PARADOXES OF MOURNING

healing your grief with three forgotten truths

ALAN D. WOLFELT, PH.D.

An imprint of the Center for Loss and Life Transition

Fort Collins, Colorado

Companion Press is an imprint of the Center for Loss and Life Transition, 3735 Broken Bow Road, Fort Collins, Colorado 80526.

29 28 27 26 25 24 23 5 4 3 2 1

ISBN: 978-1-61722-328-0

To the children, teens, adults, and families who have invited me to walk with them through the wilderness of their grief. Thank you for teaching me about the wisdom of the three Truths explored in these pages. You helped me be a "responsible rebel" and question the medical model of grief care. I am forever grateful to you for enlightening me as you entrusted me with your sacred stories of love and loss.

CONTENTS

"The more we know, the more we may be humbled by our ignorance to the point of illumination."

— Thomas Moore

INTRODUCTION

WELCOME TO THIS EXPLORATION OF THE PARADOXES OF MOURNING. As you know, a paradox is a seemingly self-contradictory statement or situation that is in fact often true. The three paradoxes of mourning we will consider together in this book might, at first glance, seem self-contradictory, but as I will reveal, they are actually three forgotten Truths with a capital T. They're Truths we must rediscover. Digging them out from the cultural basement—where we in the twenty-first century have stowed them away like Grandma's old furniture—then lovingly dusting them off and learning to appreciate them anew is a task that really can't be put off any longer. Why? Because they are essential to healing in the aftermath of significant loss.

Paradoxes are head scratchers. They often *sound* like puzzling tricks. The three we will review in the pages that follow have the seesaw of oppositional language: hello/goodbye; darkness/light; and backward/forward. But I hope to share with you the wisdom they contain—not playground games or trickery at all but instead good old-fashioned common sense.

Yes, sometimes old-fashioned trumps newfangled. Those who have walked the Earth before us have much to teach us about the best possible future, especially when it comes to the mysteries of life and death. Progress is truly wonderful, but here in the Information Age we too often mistake efficiency for effectiveness, and we are also too quick to write off ancient traditions and customs as archaic nonsense.

I am calling the three paradoxes in this book "forgotten Truths" because humankind used to know and honor them. In the many long centuries in which death was ever-present (before the twentieth century's remarkable medical advances), life was shorter but slower paced, and religious/spiritual health reigned supreme, we understood and lived the paradoxes. In fact, it is only our modern worldview that makes them seem like paradoxes at all. In the past they would simply have been life assumptions, as obvious and self-explanatory as the importance of hand washing or the fact that computers make life easier are to us today.

"Knowledge searches out and is fascinated with 'the new.' Wisdom assumes the connectedness of reality, encouraging mindfulness of 'the old'; it tends to prefer that which has endured the test of time."

— Ernest Kurtz

Before we get started, I want to clarify a couple of other key terms. When we hear the word "grief," we tend to think of death. Yes, grief is what we feel after someone we love dies, and many of you reading this book are doing so as a means of support through your bereavement. I'm so glad you've found this resource because, as a longtime grief counselor and educator, I truly believe it will help you in your journey through grief. But as you read, I also invite you to consider that we experience grief after all significant losses. Grief is what we think and feel whenever something we value is harmed or taken away. And so, we grieve after divorce.

We grieve when we are diagnosed with cancer. We grieve when our children grow up and move away. We grieve all the time, because life is replete with transitions and losses.

Mourning, on the other hand, is expressing our grief. It's grief gone public. Grief is internal, while mourning is external. The paradoxes we will explore in this book affect both grief and mourning. But mourning, as you will see, is the key to healing.

No matter which loss(es) you may have suffered, no matter how recent or how distant your significant losses, no matter your age or background or experience, if you are grieving, this book is for you. I feel honored to pull back the curtains and reveal the three paradoxical Truths of mourning to you, and I thank you for entrusting me with your time and attention. Godspeed.

Alan D. Wolfelt

May 2015

A NOTE TO BEREAVEMENT CAREGIVERS

IF YOUR LIFE'S CALLING INVOLVES HELPING PEOPLE WHO ARE GRIEVING, this book affirms the importance of your work. Mourners need you now more than ever. In days past, we as a culture embraced and lived the paradoxes of mourning. Our rituals and customs supported people through the natural and necessary process of mourning. But as we have lost wisdom about grief and the need to mourn, the application of the medical model of bereavement care has us trying to push the mourner forward with "cure" instead of "care."

Cure means to eradicate an illness. But grief is not an illness—it is a normal response to a spiritual injury. Care, on the other hand, is being present to, suffering with, and feeling with. Cure also means "to change." Caregivers often want to bring about change in people's lives. But cure can potentially damage if it does not grow out of care. Care is anchored in compassion and recognizes that this person who is hurting is my fellow human being, my brother or sister, mortal and vulnerable. And grief can never be eradicated, "gotten over," or "recovered from." It can only be experienced and, through active engagement, reconciled.

When care is our priority, there is hospitality—what Henri Nouwen described as "a sacred space where a stranger becomes a friend." As fellow beings, we don't cure but we can always care. An essential part of caring is honoring the paradoxes explored in this book. Our training puts us at risk for getting the paradoxes backward. I count you among my allies in this effort to restore compassionate, soul-based grief awareness and support to our culture. I hope you will join me in championing the Slow Grief movement (see A Final Word, page 107). And whether you are a professional caregiver or a volunteer, I thank you for the critical work you do to help your fellow human beings.

TRUTH ONE:

YOU MUST SAY HELLO
BEFORE YOU CAN
SAY GOODBYE.

"I said hello, but what I meant to say was I love you. She said goodbye, but what she probably meant to say was hello."

— Jarod Kintz

"Goodbye, my love," the husband whispers to his dying wife as her breathing slows. With her cancer in its final stage, he has known for weeks that this moment was coming. Today, the hospice staff has compassionately helped him understand that it is time. "Oh my darling," he says as he strokes her hair and kisses her forehead. "I love you so much. Goodbye..."

SUCH GOODBYES ARE ACHINGLY HARD. Whether a death is drawn-out and anticipated or sudden and unexpected, whether we are present or far away when it happens, in the aftermath we are faced with the prospect of saying goodbye. Saying goodbye hurts because it acknowledges separation. Our lives intersect with those we love. We are connected. We are companions. The ways and moments in which we connect with one another are the very essence and joy of love. But now...now we are faced with the terrible reality that we can no longer be together. We will be disconnected and apart.

Some people understand this parting as permanent and irrevocable. Others believe that the separation is temporary and that we will be rejoined with our departed loved ones after our own deaths. Regardless of your personal beliefs about the possibility of an afterlife, the separation created by death is always painful. It hurts so very much to know that for the rest of our days here on Earth, we can no longer be with, see, touch, speak to, or hear the precious person who died. As C.S. Lewis said after the death of his beloved wife, Joy, "Her absence is like the sky, spread over everything."

And yet, no matter how much we don't want to, no matter how much it hurts, when someone we love dies, we have no choice but to say goodbye. During our everyday interactions with other human beings, saying "goodbye" is a social convention. When we begin a conversation, we say "hello," and we do not take leave of the other person without first saying some form of "goodbye." To do otherwise is considered rude. We have adopted this conversational bookending as a means of acknowledging our moments of connection and separation.

> *"Breathe in: Hello moment.*
> *Breathe out: I am here."*
>
> — Meditation mantra

It is appropriate, then, that we say goodbye to those we love after they die. After all, we have become separated from them in the most profound manner possible. But unlike our daily "hellos" and "see you laters," this goodbye is not a quick send-off. Instead, it is a process that will take months and even years to unfold. When the husband in the opening paragraph whispers "goodbye" to his dying wife, he is lovingly and appropriately acknowledging the sacred moment that marks the literal transition from life to death...but at the same time he is also just embarking on the true journey of saying goodbye.

And paradoxically, the true journey of saying goodbye after the death of someone loved starts with saying hello.

SAYING HELLO TO LOVE, SAYING HELLO TO LOSS

"All you need is love," famously sang the Beatles. I couldn't agree more. We come into the world yearning to give and receive love. Authentic love is God's greatest gift to us as human beings. Love is the one human experience that invites us to feel beautifully connected and forces us to acknowledge that meaning and purpose are anchored not in isolation and aloneness, but in union and togetherness.

"'Hello' is the most powerful word against loneliness."

— Unknown

What higher purpose is there in life but to give and receive love? Love is the essence of a life of abundance and joy. No matter what life brings our way, love is our highest goal, our most passionate quest. Yes, we have a tremendous need for love—love that captures our hearts and nourishes our spirits. In fact, our capacity to give and receive love is what ultimately defines us. Nothing we have "accomplished" in our lifetimes matters as much as the ways we have loved one another.

Yet love inevitably leads to grief. You see, love and grief are two sides of the same precious coin. One does not—and cannot—exist without the other. They are the yin and yang of our lives.

People sometimes say that grief is the price we pay for the joy of having loved. This is true. This

"Every time we make the decision to love someone, we open ourselves to great suffering, because those we most love cause us not only great joy but also great pain. The greatest pain comes from leaving...the pain of the leaving can tear us apart.

"Still, if we want to avoid the suffering of leaving, we will never experience the joy of loving. And love is stronger than fear, life stronger than death, hope stronger than despair. We have to trust that the risk of loving is always worth taking."

— Henri Nouwen

also means, of course, that grief is not a universal experience. While I wish it were, sadly it is not. Grief is predicated on our capacity to give and receive love. Some people choose not to love and so never grieve. But those of us who allow ourselves the privilege—as well as the risk—of loving will also, inevitably, suffer loss.

From the moment we are born, we say hello to love in our lives by seeking it out, by acknowledging it when it unfolds, by welcoming it, and by nurturing it so that it will continue. We say, "I love you." We touch and we hug. We give of ourselves. We extend kindnesses. We revel in the giving as well as the receiving. We actively love.

"I'm for mystery, not interpretive answers... The answer is never the answer. What's really interesting is the mystery. If you seek the mystery instead of the answer, you'll always be seeking. I've never seen anybody really find the answer, but they think they have. So they stop thinking. But the job is to seek mystery, evoke mystery, plant a garden in which strange plants grow and mysteries bloom. The need for mystery is greater than the need for an answer."

— Ken Kesey

We must also say hello to loss and grief in our lives. To be sure, we do not seek it out, but when it unfolds, we must acknowledge it. I would even say that we must welcome our grief. After all, the hurt we feel is the consequence of the love we were privileged to experience. In welcoming our grief, we bear witness to the mystery of the true and full nature of love and loss.

Yes, life, love, and loss are largely mysteries. In this book I am trying to help you understand the paradoxes of mourning, but the concept of "understanding" grief harbors a paradox itself. Sometimes it is the very need to totally understand the experience of grief that can get you in trouble. For as someone once astutely observed, "Mystery is not something to be explained; it is something to be pondered."

I have found that sometimes it is in staying open to the mystery and recognizing that we don't understand and can't control everything that surrounds us that understanding eventually comes. In fact, perhaps it is "standing under" the mysterious experience of death and loss that provides us with a unique perspective: *We are not above or bigger than death.* Maybe only after exhausting the search for understanding why someone we love died can we discover a newly defined "why" for our own life.

"I want to be intelligent about mystery and not defend against it with excessive explanations and theories."

— Thomas Moore

In my experience, "understanding" comes when we *surrender*: surrender our need to compare our grief (it's not a competition); surrender our self-critical judgments (we need to be self-compassionate); and surrender our need to completely understand (we never will). The grief that touches our souls has its own voice and should not be compromised by our need for comparison, judgment, or even complete understanding. Please note that surrender is not the same as resignation. Actually, surrendering to the unknowable mystery is a courageous choice, an act of faith, a trust in God and in ourselves! We can only hold this mystery in our hearts and surround ourselves with love.

"Spiritual flexibility thrives on the reconciliation of apparent contradictions."

— David Richo

Yes, we must simultaneously "work at" and "surrender to" the grief journey. This is, in itself, a paradox. As the griever comes to know this paradox, he can, very slowly, discover the soothing of his soul. Many grievers have taught me that ultimately they find themselves wrapped in a gentle peace—the peace of living at once in the encounter ("the grief work") and the surrender (embracing the mystery of not fully knowing or understanding).

"What complicates our stories is that one part of our dignity as human beings, our ability to *do*, tends to outrun our *be*-ing. We love to manipulate, to bring about, to control... But our *be*-ing is more important, and there are some realities...we cannot control."

— Ernest Kurtz

Buddhism teaches that there are four noble truths. The first of these truths is called the truth of *dukkha*—a Sanskrit word that means "suffering" or "unsatisfactoriness." In our lives, we experience *dukkha* in several ways. We suffer through aging, illness, and dying. We suffer by holding onto things that are constantly changing (loss). And we suffer because everything is impermanent. In essence, sorrow, grief, and despair are *dukkha*.

Dukkha is unavoidable in life says the first noble truth of Buddhism. And paradoxically, acknowledging this—acknowledging loss's inextricable nature and constant presence—is the first step to easing the suffering it causes. Likewise, saying hello to the reality of your loss is the first step in saying goodbye, which is the process of grief and mourning, which in turn will eventually ease your suffering.

Despite what our grief-avoiding culture would have you believe, you cannot begin to say goodbye until you first say hello. This is one of the three forgotten Truths of grief and mourning.

> **"Our deepest ethical and spiritual wisdom calls us not only to watch vigilantly over the bodies of the living but also to care tenderly for the bodies of the dead. So why don't we do it? Curiously, we are becoming the first society in the world for whom the dead are no longer required—or desired—at their own funerals."**
>
> — Thomas G. Long and Thomas Lynch

SAYING HELLO TO THE PHYSICAL REALITY OF DEATH

In centuries past, our actions and rituals made it clear that we understood the necessity of saying hello to the reality of death.

In ancient Greece—hundreds of years before Christ—relatives of the person who died washed and anointed the body with oil, dressed the body, and placed it on a bed. When the body was ready, relatives and friends came to mourn and pay respects. Next, the body was carried to the cemetery in a procession just before dawn. The body was placed in a grave that was marked by a mound or marble statue.

Similar rituals have also long been carried out by many cultures across the globe. We have always—from the time of Neanderthals, even, anthropologists suggest—honored the body of the person who died through the moment it is laid in its final resting place.

Here in the United States, it wasn't that long ago that we practiced essentially the same rituals. Up until the early 1900s, those we loved usually died at home, and we sat at their bedsides and held their hands as they did so. Over and over—for death was an everyday occurrence in the centuries before vaccines, antibiotics, and safe surgery—we literally bore witness to death. Then, after death, we cared for the dead ourselves. We washed the precious bodies of the people we loved, dressed them, and laid them out for viewing in our own parlors.

> "Grief work...is not so much the brain's to do, as the body's. And it is better done by large muscles than gray matter; less the burden of cerebral synapse and more of shoulders, shared embraces, sore hearts."
>
> — Thomas G. Long and Thomas Lynch

Next we sat vigil. The term "wake" comes from the Middle English *waken*, meaning "to be awake, to keep watch." In days gone by, it was customary to keep around-the-clock vigil over the dead bodies of those we loved. We took turns with other family members sitting at our loved ones' sides, 24 hours a day, to safeguard their bodies, offer prayers, pay respects, receive friends, and comfort one another. In the Jewish faith, the time of the person's death until the burial is called *aninut*. During *aninut*, the mourners' sole focus and responsibility is caring for the person who died.

Today, of course, death often happens in hospitals, and the dead bodies of the people we love are almost always stored at funeral homes from the time of the removal of the bodies from their place of death until the time of the funeral. Death happens or is pronounced in a clinical setting, and dead bodies are handled by professionals behind closed doors. Essentially, our current practices of body handling encourage us to skip saying hello to the reality of the death.

"They took my mother's body away so quickly. There we all were, touching her, hugging her, kissing her, saying goodbye… Her being seemed present. I could feel it hovering at the ceiling of the room, changing, but not gone. I could have spent days with the body, getting used to it, loving it, saying goodbye to it."

— Megan O'Rourke

Also in days gone by, the body of the person who died was the focal part of the entire funeral process, from the procession into the church to the procession out of the church to the procession to the cemetery through to the burial. The body never for a moment left the family's sight—or heart.

In recent decades, conversely, the trend has been toward body-absent funeral ceremonies. Today, bodies are often cremated immediately, often without loved ones having spent time with them or even having looked at them beforehand. When my mother died at the age of 83, my family made the wise but out-of-fashion decision to have two days of visitation, with her body on display in an open casket. During the visitation hours, my family and I received many old friends, activating community support. But what I found striking was that when people approached her body in the casket, over and over again their first reaction was to say, out loud, "Oh, she's really dead." Others said, "She looks so nice." Both responses, which I've found to be common reactions at open-casket visitations, are forms of saying hello. "Oh, she's really dead" means "Oh, hello, dead version of the person I used to know when she was alive." "She looks so nice" means "She doesn't look alive. She looks dead. But I can see that dead isn't creepy. It is normal and natural." While historically we understood the essential, universal need to honor and affirm the life of the person who died with the body present throughout the entire funeral process, now the guest of honor is often missing in action.

> **"Ours is a species that down the millennia has learned to process grief by processing the objects of our grief, the bodies of the dead, from one place to the next. We bear mortality by bearing mortals—the living and the dead—to the brink of a uniquely changed reality: Heaven or Valhalla or Whatever Is Next… Whatever afterlife there is or isn't, human beings have marked their ceasing to be by going the distance with their dead—to the tomb or the fire or the grave, the holy tree or the deep sea, whatever sacred space of oblivion we consign them to. And we've been doing this since the beginning."**
>
> — Thomas G. Long and Thomas Lynch

In a recent blog post exemplifying our current cultural misunderstanding about skipping hello, a Chicago reporter made the claim that funeral processions from the location of the funeral to the cemetery are "a traffic hazard…a massive inconvenience… and completely useless." What he, and our culture in general, has forgotten is that the cortège, which literally means "to pay honor," is not about funeral attendees finding their way to the cemetery without getting lost. Instead, it is intended to activate community support, acknowledge the death of a neighbor, and provide a sense of solidarity to those in the procession. Yes, processions do slow down traffic and force us to pause when we may be in a hurry. They are supposed to. They make us say hello to the physical reality of death.

If you have ever watched someone die, cared for a dead body, or visited the body of a loved one in an open casket, you have said hello to the reality of that person's death. I believe the more time you spent bearing witness to and even feeling the fact of their death with your own two hands, the more deeply you were able to acknowledge the reality of their death.

Human beings are, of course, capable of abstract thought. We can hear the news of the death of someone loved, and even if we never see the dead body, we understand the fact of the death. In this sense, death is an abstract concept. But at the same time, death is a physical reality—one we can take in through our five senses. It is true that the believing that follows seeing is stronger than the believing that is strictly conceptual. When we say hello to the reality of the death of someone loved by spending time with the body, not only are we honoring the body that animated the singular life of a person who was precious to us, we are also helping our minds and ultimately our hearts embark on the journey to goodbye.

I hope you were privileged to spend time with the body of the person who died. Yet if you were not—it is not always a possibility—rest assured that there are other ways to say hello to the reality of the death. We'll discuss those next.

SAYING HELLO TO THE REALITY OF THE DEATH AFTER THE FUNERAL

Seeing and spending time with the body of the person who died before burial or cremation is one important way to say hello to the reality of the death. But in the weeks that follow, you must continue to find ways to say hello.

Think of it this way: the death of someone you love opens the door onto a new existential reality. Naturally, it's a reality that you don't *want* to enter, and some degree of shock, numbness, and denial are normal and even necessary in the very early days after the death. To survive, you may continue to try to push away the reality at times. I refer to this as the evade-encounter dance. But slowly, gently, and in doses, you must step through the door. You must open your eyes and heart to the new reality.

> "A yes to feelings is a station stop before we get to philosophical explanations, theological consolations, or encouraging maxims."
>
> — David Richo

Being honest with yourself about your grief is one way you continue to say hello. Remember, grief is what you think and feel on the inside after you experience a loss. Find a place to be quiet and alone with your thoughts and feelings. In these moments of solitude, learn to check in with yourself about the death. Ask yourself, "What am I thinking and feeling right now about this loss?" Allow your thoughts and feelings to surface without judgment. Look your grief in the face and say hello to it.

In the Buddhist tradition, the concept of *bodhicitta*, which means "awakened heart," teaches us that it is essential for us to not be afraid of who we really are or how we are feeling. Instead, we must awaken to the truth of our own thoughts and feelings. We must, in other words, say hello to them.

The word "feeling" comes from an Indo-European root that means "touch." When you have feelings, you are being touched by something that has happened (or that you think might happen). Remember this concept of being touched as you say hello to your grief. It is touching you. It is reaching out to you. It is tapping you on the shoulder—and sometimes punching you in the gut. Look at it. Feel it. Say hello to it and befriend it.

"Nature made us feel
so we could evolve."

— David Richo

The next level of hello after a death is the expression of the authentic thoughts and feelings you have allowed to surface. Expressing grief is called mourning, and mourning is essential to your eventual healing. And learning to express your grief—especially if you are not naturally comfortable with sharing your innermost thoughts and feelings—is how you say hello to the need to mourn.

What's more, mourning is the public hello we give to our grief. It is the coming out with our truth. "Attention!" we say. "Something important happened to me. I loved and I lost. Now I am broken. World, say hello to my inner experience of grief. Grief, say hello to the world."

"Our grief, though naturally difficult,
is a source of energy within us.
When we outwardly mourn,
we unleash this amazing
healing force."

— Alan D. Wolfelt, Ph.D.

Essentially, mourning is grief in action. We talked about love in action—saying "I love you," hugging and touching, giving of ourselves, extending kindnesses. Mourning is the equivalent after loss. Just as love without action is unfulfilling and unsustainable, loss without mourning is a dead end. We shut ourselves off from life and loving when we do not mourn. We die while we are alive. (More on carried grief on page 97.) But when we find the courage to *act*ivate our grief, we create the movement that carries us forward and through.

"People who talk at grief,
instead of holding hands with grief,
are a menace. Words come later,
but only after tears."

— John Bowker

In addition to talking to friends and family about your grief, you mourn by:

- journaling
- crying
- participating in a support group
- seeing a grief counselor
- displaying photos and other tangible reminders of the person who died
- creating artwork
- volunteering
- making ongoing use of ritual

As you find ways to outwardly and actively mourn that help you, try also to notice your own resistance. When you feel yourself resisting the need to do the work of mourning—because it's too painful, because it's too hard, because you're too tired, because you'd rather distract yourself with something entertaining—acknowledge your resistance. Say hello to your resistance. If you're resisting because it's time to take a break, then by all means, take a break. Grief and mourning must be dosed. But if you find that in actuality you're resisting in an attempt to go around instead of through, acknowledge the resistance then reach out for help. Tell a friend or counselor about your struggles to say hello to your loss. Saying hello to your resistance in this open and active way will help you move toward saying hello to your loss openly and actively as well.

"The well with no bottom always has a bottom, but we must swing down there to see it."

— Unknown

SAYING HELLO TO THE NEW SELF YOU ARE BECOMING

Loving someone changes us forever. So does losing them.

After the death of someone loved, we are different than we were before the death. We are injured, and while we can work to heal the injury, it will forever leave a scar that marks both the love and the loss.

> **"The real problem has far less to do with *what is really out there* than it does with our *resistance to finding out what is really out there*. The suffering comes from our reluctance to learn to walk in the dark."**
>
> — Barbara Brown Taylor

We have said that before you can begin the true journey of saying goodbye, you must say hello to the reality of the loss. You must also say hello to your grief, both honestly acknowledging your thoughts and feelings to yourself and then finding ways to express them. And as you acknowledge and express your loss, you will naturally begin to realize that you are changing. Along the way, say hello to the new you.

You see, your self-identity will change. Your personal identity, or self-perception, is the result of the ongoing process of establishing a sense of who you are. Part of your self-identity comes from the relationships you have with other people. When someone with whom you have a relationship dies, your self-identity, or the way you see yourself, naturally changes.

> *"Not until we are lost do we begin to understand ourselves."*
>
> — Henry David Thoreau

You may have gone from being a "wife" or "husband" to a "widow" or "widower." You may have gone from being a "parent" to a "bereaved parent." The way you define yourself and the way society defines you is changed. As one woman said, "I used to have a husband and was part of a couple. Now I'm not only single but a single parent and a widow...I hate that word."

A death often requires you to take on new roles that had been filled by the person who died. After all, someone still has to take out the garbage, someone still has to buy the groceries, someone still has to balance the checkbook. You confront your changed identity every time you do something that used to be done by or with the person who died. This can be very hard work and, at times, can leave you feeling very drained of emotional, physical, and spiritual energy.

> "To lead a more passionate, full, and delightful life, we must realize that we can endure a lot of pain and pleasure for the sake of finding out who we are and what this work is, how we tick and how our world ticks, how the whole thing just *is*."
>
> — Pema Chodron

The person who died was a part of you. This death means you mourn a loss not only outside of yourself, but inside of yourself as well. I often say that we love from the outside in, but we mourn from the inside out. At times, overwhelming sadness and loneliness may be your constant companions. You may feel that when this person died, part of you died with him or her. And now you are faced with finding some meaning in going on with your life even though you may often feel so empty.

You may occasionally feel child-like as you struggle with your changing identity. You may feel a temporarily heightened dependence on others as well as feelings of helplessness, frustration, inadequacy, and fear. These feelings can be overwhelming and scary, but they are actually a natural response to this process of saying hello to the new you you are becoming.

Yes, when we befriend our feelings, which are the essence of our humanity, we are transformed. Many mourners discover that as they transform—and stop now and then to acknowledge the changes they see—they ultimately discover some positive aspects of their changed self-identity. You may develop a renewed confidence in yourself, for example. You may develop a more caring, kind, and sensitive part of yourself. You may develop an assertive part of your identity that empowers you to go on living even though you continue to feel a sense of loss.

Another aspect of the changing you that you must stop and say hello to along the way has to do with your understanding of the meaning and purpose of life. Before this death, you held a set of spiritual beliefs—whether religious, humanist, agnostic, atheist, or a combination. The death of someone loved naturally plunges you into a period of questioning your worldview. You will likely examine your philosophy of life and explore religious and spiritual values. You may discover yourself searching for meaning in your continued living as you ask "Why?" and "How?" questions. "Why did this happen now, in this way?" "How will I survive this?" You may notice that your "Why?" questions will often come first, before you can move forward enough to start thinking about "How?" questions.

"In the depth of winter, I found that there was in me an invincible summer."

— Albert Camus

This death calls for you to confront your own spirituality. You may doubt your faith and have spiritual conflicts and questions racing through your head and heart. This is normal and part of your journey toward renewed living.

You might feel distant from your God or higher power, even questioning the very existence of God. You may rage at your God. Such feelings of doubt and anger are normal. Remember—mourners often find themselves questioning their faith for months and years before they rediscover meaning in life. But be assured: It can be done, even when you don't have all the answers.

Early in your grief, allow yourself to openly mourn without pressuring yourself to have answers to such profound "meaning of life" questions. Move at your own pace as you recognize that allowing yourself to hurt and finding meaning are not mutually exclusive. More often your need to mourn and find meaning in your continued living will blend into each other, with the former giving way to the latter as healing occurs.

SAYING GOODBYE

We've already talked a little about the idea of saying goodbye to someone who has died. Not only is it a natural impulse, it's a social ritual, and it's also something our culture expects of us and we expect of ourselves. But even if we have the privilege of saying goodbye in the moments right before or after death or in the chaotic days before the burial or cremation, it's essential to

A WORD OF CAUTION ABOUT SAYING GOODBYE

When someone we love is actively dying, sometimes we are encouraged to tell them that it is OK with us if they go or that they should "go toward the light."

I know that it is hard to watch someone you love die a painful, lingering death. It is normal and natural to want their suffering to end. But I would also like you to consider that saying goodbye prematurely, or trying to push someone who is dying through the door, is often a reflection of our modern discomfort and impatience with the dying process. We would rather not say such an extended hello to what it can be like when a human body dies, so we try to hurry it along.

I believe that we should spend more time saying hello to the person who is dying—something we were better at doing in generations past. Instead of rushing to goodbye, we can spend those precious last weeks and days sharing our memories and expressing our love. Hello is anchored in love, while goodbye is anchored in logic. The dying person's body came into this world when it was ready, and it will also leave this world when it is ready.

While some dying people do ask for our permission to make the transition, most do not need our permission or encouragement. Let the dying go when are ready to go—not when we are ready. In the meantime, let's keep saying hello.

remember that saying goodbye to someone we love is actually not a single moment in time but rather a never-ending process.

"You've changed me forever. And I'll never forget you."

— Kiera Cass

Grief never truly ends because love never ends. People do not "get over" grief because they do not "get over" the love that caused the grief. After someone we love dies, we step through a doorway into a new reality, but we never fully close and lock the door behind us.

"Love doesn't die with death. Love is like liquid; when it pours out, it seeps into others' lives. Love changes form and shape. Love gets into everything. Death doesn't conquer all; love does. Love wins every single time. Love wins by lasting through death. Love wins by loving more, loving again, loving without fear."

— Kate O'Neill

Still, if you say hello to your loss, grief, mourning, and changing self in all the ways we've reviewed in this chapter, over time and with the support of others you will more and more come to find that you have ultimately said a kind of final goodbye to the person who died. No, you do not forget, get over, resolve, or recover from the death, but you become reconciled to it. Reconciliation literally means "to make life good again." In reconciliation, you come to integrate the new reality of moving forward in life without the physical presence of the person who died. With reconciliation comes a renewed sense of energy and confidence and a capacity to become re-involved in the activities of living. There is also an acknowledgment that pain and grief are difficult, yet necessary, parts of life.

"You will lose someone you can't live without, and your heart will be badly broken, and the bad news is that you never completely get over the loss of your beloved. But this is also the good news. They live forever in your broken heart that doesn't seal back up. And you come through. It's like having a broken leg that never heals perfectly—that still hurts when the weather gets cold, but you learn to dance with the limp."

— Anne Lamott

As the experience of reconciliation unfolds, you will recognize that life is and will continue to be different without the presence of the person who died. Changing the relationship with the person who died from one of presence to one of memory and redirecting one's energy and initiative toward the future often takes longer—and involves more hard work—than most people are aware.

We come to reconciliation in our grief journeys when the full reality of the death becomes a part of us. Beyond an intellectual working through of the death, there is also an emotional and spiritual working through. What had been understood at the "head" level is now also understood at the "heart" level.

You will find that as you achieve reconciliation, the sharp, ever-present pain of grief will give rise to a renewed sense of meaning and purpose. Your feelings of loss will not completely disappear, yet they will soften, and the intense pangs of grief will become less frequent. Hope for a continued life will emerge as you are able to make commitments to the future, realizing that the person you have given love to and received love from will never be forgotten. The unfolding of this journey is not intended to create a return to an "old normal" but instead the discovery of a "new normal."

Signs that you are reconciling the loss will include

- A recognition of the reality and finality of the death.
- A return to stable eating and sleeping patterns.
- A renewed sense of release from the person who died. You will still have thoughts about the person, but you will not be preoccupied by these thoughts.
- The capacity to enjoy experiences in life that are normally enjoyable.
- The establishment of new and healthy relationships.
- The capacity to live a full life without feelings of guilt or lack of self-respect.
- The drive to organize and plan one's life toward the future.
- The serenity to become comfortable with the way things are rather than attempting to make things as they were.
- The versatility to welcome more change in life.
- The acquaintance of new parts of yourself that you have discovered in your grief journey.
- The adjustment to new role changes and a new self.
- The acknowledgment that the pain of loss is an inherent part of life resulting from the ability to give and receive love.

Reconciliation emerges much in the way grass grows. Usually we don't check our lawns daily to see if the grass is growing, but it does grow, and soon we come to realize it's time to mow the grass again. Likewise, we don't look at ourselves each day as mourners to see how we are healing. Yet we do come to realize, over the course of months and years, that we have come a long way.

"There was no sudden, striking, and emotional transition. Like the warming of a room or the coming of daylight, when you first notice them they have already been going on for some time."

— C.S. Lewis

On the road to reconciliation, there is usually not one great moment of "arrival," but instead subtle changes and small advancements. It's helpful to have gratitude for even tiny signs of progress. If you are beginning to taste your food again, be thankful. If you mustered the energy to meet your friend for lunch, be grateful. If you finally got a good night's sleep, rejoice.

Of course, you will take some steps backward from time to time, but that is to be expected. (More on that in Truth Three.) Keep believing in yourself. Set your intention to reconcile your grief and have hope that you can and will come to live and love again.

Along the road to reconciliation, if you are openly, honestly, and actively mourning, you will be saying lots of hellos. Oh hello, this death. Oh hello, this thought. Oh hello, this feeling. Oh hello, this change. Oh hello, this me. Oh hello, this doubt. Oh hello, this new belief. But you will also be saying many goodbyes. Goodbye, this voice, this kiss, this body. Goodbye, this routine. Goodbye, this me. Goodbye, this belief. Goodbye, this ever-present pain.

Your hellos and goodbyes will overlap one another, with more hellos needed at the start of your journey and more goodbyes in the later days.

Saying goodbye is not the same as "closure." As I said, you never fully close the door on the love and grief you feel for someone who has died. But you can achieve a sense of peace. The days of intense and constant turmoil can be replaced by serene acceptance as well as days of love, hope, and joy.

So yes, work on saying your goodbyes. But first, work on saying your hellos.

TRUTH TWO:

YOU MUST MAKE FRIENDS
WITH THE DARKNESS
BEFORE YOU CAN
ENTER THE LIGHT.

"In a dark time,
the eye begins to see."

— Theodore Roethke

BEFORE THE INVENTION AND WIDESPREAD adoption of electricity, we lived much of our lives in the dark. For millennia, human beings awoke and became active when the sun rose and stopped to rest when the sun set. Of course, fires, torches, and candles provided some light during the night, but for the most part, darkness prevailed for many long hours every 24-hour period.

Can you imagine life before electricity? No kitchen lights in the evening. No glowing computer or TV screens. No bedside lamps. Outside, no streetlights. No lit store signs. Think back to the last power outage you experienced in your home or neighborhood or to your last camping trip in the wilderness. At night—everywhere, nothing but deep, inky blackness.

"Whoever you are: some evening take a step out of your house, which you know so well. Enormous space is near."

— Rainer Maria Rilke

We used to know the dark. It was as much a part of our lives as the light. And in the darkness we could marvel at the stars, tell stories to one another, contemplate life and death, and sink into restorative sleep. We sat in the darkness, and as our eyes grew accustomed to it, we could see its unique shapes, shadows, and qualities. Yes, we were vulnerable in the dark, but we were also stilled and one with each other and with the universe in a way impossible during the busyness of our sunlit days.

The International Dark-Sky Association is a nonprofit "fighting to preserve the night." Recognizing that human-produced light creates "light pollution" that diminishes our view of the stars, disrupts our circadian rhythms as well as ecosystems, and wastes significant amounts of energy, the association seeks to reserve the use of artificial lighting at night to only what is truly necessary.

I have a home in Arizona in a neighborhood that embraces this policy. Only very minimal artificial outdoor lighting is allowed. The blackness of the night there has given me a new appreciation for spending time in the dark. This is where I go to renew myself when I am worn out and weary. I look up at the millions of stars in the sky—so much more visible there than they are anywhere else I typically spend time—and I know that it is only in the darkness that we can discover the light. I ponder the mysteries of the universe. I am at peace. I am restored.

As you read about Truth Two, I would like you to remember this mantra of "fighting to preserve the night." During our times of grief, we are also well served to fight to honor and preserve the sanctity and restorative powers of the dark night of the soul.

THE DARK NIGHT OF THE SOUL

One way in which we used to honor the need to make friends with the darkness of grief was to observe a period of mourning. During this time—whose length and detailed customs varied by era, religion, and culture as well as by each mourner's specific relationship to the person who died—mourners essentially withdrew from society. They did not attend parties or social functions, although they did receive friends in their home. When they

"For now we see through a glass, darkly, but then face to face. Now I know in part; but then shall I know, even as also I am known."

— 1 Corinthians 13:12

did venture out into the community, they wore clothing that outwardly represented their internal reality. In Europe the custom of wearing black clothing during a time of grief dates back to the Roman Empire. Other cultures have also dictated mourning dress. In India mourners wore white, while in parts of Asia mourners wore indigo or red. Interestingly, abating grief in some cultures has been signaled by a color change in clothing, such as moving from all black clothing to black-and-white clothing and finally to gray or lavender.

Such mourning "rules" or customs were a way of acknowledging loss and honoring the need for a period of darkness. They were signs of a deeply profound, spiritual crisis. Because while grief affects all aspects of our lives—our physical, cognitive, emotional, social, and spiritual selves—it is fundamentally a spiritual journey. In fact, a significant loss plunges you into what C.S. Lewis, Eckhart Tolle, and various Christian mystics have called "the dark night of the soul."

"We found this pattern repeated on the level of human creativity: the scientist, faced by a perplexing situation—Kepler's discrepant eight-minute arc, Einstein's light-traveler paradox—must plunge into a 'dark night of the soul' before he can reemerge into the light. The history of the sciences and arts is a tale of recurrent crises, of traumatic challenges, which entail a temporary disintegration of the traditional forms of reasoning and perception...(and) a new innocence of the eye; followed by the liberation from restraint of creative potentials, and their reintegration in a new synthesis."

— Arthur Koestler

The first use of the phrase "the dark night of the soul" was in the sixteenth-century poem of that title written by Roman Catholic mystic Saint John of the Cross. He began writing the poem during the year he spent in a monastery prison—many months of that in a solitary confinement as black as night. The poem tells the story of the soul's journey after death as it makes its way back to God. Along the way, the soul is challenged by hardships and difficulties. The poem is a metaphor for the human soul's often painful and torturous journey in life. What Saint John is saying in the poem is that the darkness is a gift. It strips away our pretensions and our lies and makes possible a truer relationship with God.

"In the book of Genesis, darkness was first; light came second."

— Barbara Brown Taylor

After the death of someone loved, the dark night of the soul can be a long and very black night indeed. If you are struggling after a significant loss of any kind, you are probably inhabiting that long, dark night. It is uncomfortable and scary. It hurts. Yet if you allow yourself to sit still in the blackness without trying to fight it, deny it, or run away from it, you will find that it has something to teach you.

A person died and stood before God.

God asked, "Where are your wounds?"

The person answered, "What wounds? I have none."

God said, "Was there nothing worth fighting for?"

THE SO-CALLED DARK EMOTIONS

Have you ever noticed that we tend to equate the dark with all things evil and bad, while light represents goodness and purity? Darkness is night, ghosts, caves, bats, devils, and vampires. Darkness is also ignorance and void. And when we feel "dark" emotions, we mean that we feel sadness, emptiness, loss, depression, despair, shame, and fear.

Yes, the dark emotions are painful and challenging to experience. But are they really "bad"? No, they are not.

Feelings are not intrinsically good or bad—they simply are. They arise in us in response to what we are seeing, hearing, touching, tasting, and smelling in any given moment. They also emanate more abstractly, from our thoughts. Feelings are essentially the bodily response to the existential experience of living and being.

Another way of thinking of them is that they are the method with which our souls communicate with our minds and bodies (and perhaps vice versa). Our feelings are always necessary. We should always pay attention to them, for they are there to teach us something.

> *"To learn to attend is a beginning. To learn to attend more and more deeply is the path itself."*
>
> — John Tarrant

And so we must turn to the dark emotions of grief. We must acknowledge them and allow ourselves to feel them. In fact, I often say that we must befriend our dark emotions. Befriending pain is hard. It's true that it is easier to avoid, repress, or deny the pain of grief than it is to embrace it, yet it is in befriending our pain that we learn from it and unlock our capacity to be transformed by it.

Still, you will probably discover that you need to dose yourself in embracing your pain. In other words, you cannot (nor should you try to) overload yourself with the hurt all at one time. Sometimes you may need to distract yourself from the pain of loss, while at other times you will need to create a safe place to move toward it.

"For centuries, melancholy has been seen as a characteristic mood of the soul... From our devotion to more spiritual feelings such as joy and excitement, we may undervalue this emotion and may even try to find ways of banishing it."

— Thomas Moore

Feeling your pain can sometimes zap you of your energy. When your energy is low, you may be tempted to suppress your grief or even run from it. If you start running and keep running, you may never heal. Dose your pain: yes! Deny your pain: no!

"Psychological wholeness and spiritual holiness never exclude the problem from the solution. If it is wholeness, then it is always paradoxical, and holds both the dark and light states of things."

— Richard Rohr

As you encounter your pain, you will also need to nurture yourself physically, emotionally, and spiritually. Eat well, rest often, and exercise regularly. Find others with whom you can share your painful thoughts and feelings; friends who listen without judging are your most important helpers as you befriend your pain. Never forget that grief is a process, not an event. Your pain will probably ebb and flow for months, even years; embracing it when it washes over you will require patience, support, and strength.

Unfortunately, our culture today tends to encourage the denial of pain. Forgetting the Truth about darkness, we misunderstand the role of suffering. If you openly express your feelings of grief, misinformed friends may advise you to "carry on" or "keep your chin up." If, on the other hand, you remain "strong" and "in control," you may be congratulated for "doing well" with your grief. Actually, doing well with your grief means becoming well acquainted with your pain.

The trend toward memorial services that do not include the body of the person who died and that focus on "celebration of life" instead of the dark emotions is one blatant example of our culture's attempt to circumvent normal and necessary pain. Increasingly we're having parties instead of funerals. Recently a distraught woman came to see me who had been intentionally excluded from the "funeral party" her family was planning for her favorite uncle. As they explained to her, they knew she was close to him and would cry at the funeral; therefore, she would not be allowed to attend. To borrow a phrase from the musical group R.E.M., we "shiny, happy people" have forgotten that the true purpose of a funeral is to befriend and express our darkness in the company of others who feel it as well so that we can support one another.

"What hurts you, blesses you.
Darkness is your candle."

— Rumi

We also encourage the treating away of pain with drugs like antidepressants. While clinical depression is real and antidepressants are sometimes necessary, too often we use them as a means of circumventing the normal and necessary pain of human existence. If you take a pill to enter the light without ever befriending the darkness—especially if you are using antidepressants without concurrent talk therapy—you are simply inviting carried grief (see page 97).

In your reading, you might also encounter "the new science of loss." In the past decade or so, some researchers and pop-science writers have begun making the claim that people are born programmed to get over grief. We don't need to fully embrace or express our dark emotions, they are wont to say. Instead, we are resilient creatures, and our grief will often go away on its own. The problem is, such thinking is the product of our contemporary culture's denial of the necessity of darkness. Its scientific posturing belies the spiritual nature of grief and mourning. In the throes of the technological age, I know that it's tempting to want to rely on science and technology, but the hard sciences have little to teach us about what is better thought of as "the old art of loss."

"There's a common misunderstanding among all human beings who have ever been born on the earth that the best way to live is to try to avoid pain and just try to get comfortable."

— Pema Chodron

In fact, I am in search of understanding that has nothing to do with quantitative studies and evidence-based therapies. Something happens to grief when a culture is drawn to science and leaves art behind. Grief becomes something to be resolved or overcome instead of experienced. When we lose a sense of mystery, we are seduced into wanting to get rid of grief symptoms as quickly as possible. In the most recent edition of the *Diagnostic and Statistical Manual of Mental Disorders* (called the DSM for short), published by the American Psychiatric Association, major depression can now be diagnosed when common grief symptoms such as depressed mood, finding little pleasure in activities, and loss of energy are present for only two weeks.

"There is no sun without shadow, and it is essential to know the night."

— Albert Camus

In her book *Healing Through The Dark Emotions*, author and psychotherapist Miriam Greenspan, who herself became well acquainted with grief when her son was born with a serious brain injury and died before he could ever leave the hospital, advises a three-step process of dealing with dark emotions: Attending, Befriending, and Surrendering (ABS). Attending means feeling them in the body, acknowledging their presence, and naming them. Befriending means allowing them to be present. "You don't try to suppress, dispel, avoid, deny, analyze, or distract yourself from them," writes Greenspan. "Nor do you melodramatically indulge or mindlessly vent them." Instead, you simply maintain a mindful awareness of them. And finally, Surrendering means letting the emotions flow through you until they (not you) have run their course.

The pain of the dark night of the soul can seem intolerable, and yet the only way to emerge into the light of a new morning is to first experience the night. As a wise person once observed, "Darkness is the chair upon which light sits."

CLEAN PAIN VERSUS DIRTY PAIN

While embracing the dark emotions is necessary on the journey to healing, only "clean pain" needs attention. "Dirty pain," once identified, can be safely separated out and ignored, leaving you with more psychic energy to embrace only the pain that truly needs embracing.

> *"Just as the night makes the day so jubilant, our darkness is the deliverance to true spiritual understanding."*
>
> — Margaret Reckling

What's the difference? "Clean pain" is the normal pain that follows difficult life experiences. "Dirty pain" is the damaging, multiplied pain we create when we catastrophize, judge ourselves, or allow ourselves to be judged by others. Dirty pain is the story we tell ourselves about the clean pain.

> **"Stand still. The trees ahead and bushes beside you**
>
> **Are not lost. Wherever you are is called Here,**
>
> **And you must treat it as a powerful stranger,**
>
> **Must ask permission to know it and be known."**
>
> — David Wagoner

When someone we love dies, for example, we naturally experience grief. That is clean pain. But when we become frozen by worry that we did something wrong, or when we assume that others think badly of us (when in fact we don't really know what they think), or when we feel like we "should" be doing something differently than we are and so feel bad about it, we're experiencing dirty pain.

As you work to make friends with the darkness, try to discern your clean pain from your dirty pain. Most of us experience both, but learning to tell the two apart can help us be kinder to ourselves as well as more effective in our journey.

THE NECESSITY OF GRIEF

Yes, when you are grieving, it is necessary to feel sadness and other so-called dark emotions. But *why* is it necessary? Why does emotional pain have to exist at all? Couldn't we just move from loss to shock to acceptance without all that pain in the middle?

The answer is that sadness plays an essential role. It forces us to regroup—physically, cognitively, emotionally, socially, and spiritually. When we are sad, we instinctively turn inward. We withdraw. We slow down. It's as if our soul presses the pause button and says, "Whoa, whoa, whoaaa. Time out. I need to acknowledge what's happened here and really consider what I want to do next." The renowned Jungian psychologist James Hillman said it this way: "Instead of seeing depression as a dysfunction, it is a functioning phenomenon. It stops you cold, sets you down, makes you damn miserable. So you know it functions."

> **"Ending—neutral zone—new beginning. People make the new beginning only if they have first made an ending and spent some time in the neutral zone."**
>
> — William Bridges

In fact, many of the acute symptoms of grief force us to slow down. We experience "anhedonia," which means the inability to find pleasure in activities that we used to enjoy. In other words, we don't feel like doing *anything*. We also tend to feel tired and sluggish. We are listless emotionally as well as physically. Our limbs feel heavy. This is called "the lethargy of grief." And we have trouble focusing. We start things but can't seem to finish them. We're easily distracted. Such polyphasic behavior slows us down as well.

Yet many of the messages that people in grief are given contradict the need for depression, withdrawal, and stillness: "Carry on"; "Keep busy"; "I have someone for you to meet." The catch-22 for many grievers is that as they try to frantically move forward, they often lose their way.

"Be still. Stillness reveals the secrets of eternity."

— Lao Tzu

Times of stillness are not anchored in a psychological need but in a spiritual necessity. A lack of stillness hastens confusion and disorientation and results in a waning of the spirit. If you do not rest in stillness for a time, you cannot and will not find your way out of the wilderness of grief.

Stillness allows for the transition from "soul work" to "spirit work." According to the groundbreaking thinking of Carl Jung, "soul work" is the downward movement of the psyche. It is the willingness to connect with what is dark, deep, and not necessarily pleasant. "Spirit work," on the other hand, involves the upward, ascending movement of the psyche. It is during spirit work that you find renewed meaning and joy in life.

Soul work comes before spirit work. Soul work lays the ground for spirit work. The spirit cannot ascend until the soul first descends.

Even Jesus had to descend down to hell before he could ascend up to heaven. The withdrawal, slowing down, and stillness of the dark emotions create the conditions necessary for soul work.

> *"One does not become enlightened by imagining figures of light but by making the darkness conscious."*
>
> — Carl Jung

This very ability to consider our own existence is, in fact, what defines us as human beings. Unlike other animals, we are self-aware. And to be self-aware is to feel sadness but also joy and timeless love.

I sometimes call the necessary darkness of grief "sitting in your wound." When you sit in the wound of your grief, you surrender to it. You acquiesce to the instinct to slow down and turn inward. You allow yourself to appropriately wallow in the pain. You shut the world out for a time so that, eventually, you have created space to let the world back in.

THE DARKNESS OF LIMINAL SPACE

Grief lives in liminal space. *Limina* is the Latin word for threshold, the space betwixt and between. When you are in liminal space—or limbo—you are not busily and unthinkingly going about your daily life. Neither are you living from a place of assuredness about your relationships and beliefs. Instead, you are unsettled. Both your automatic daily routine and your core beliefs have been shaken, forcing you to reconsider who you are, why you're here, and what life means.

Notice that the experience of liminal space requires patience. Most of us are uneasy with waiting, with *not doing,* with *in betweenness.* Our culture, which is preoccupied with getting us to "let go," "move on," and "get closure," is equally impatient. But making friends with the shadowland of limbo does not happen quickly and efficiently. In fact, if we attempt to quickly get out of liminal space, we can sabotage our real healing.

"A pearl is a beautiful thing that is produced by an injured life. It is the tear [that results] from the injury of the oyster. The treasure of our being in this world is also produced by an injured life. If we had not been wounded, if we had not been injured, then we will not produce the pearl."

— Stephan Hoeller

"Despair is a time of waiting, of paralysis, of non-time. When we are in its kingdom we do not distinguish among things. Our experience is incomplete because it is non-experience; it is not anything in particular itself and neither is it turning into something else."

— John Tarrant

The concept of convalescence also applies here. A significant loss is an injury to our physical, cognitive, emotional, social, and spiritual selves. Just as after a significant physical injury, we must rest and convalesce, which connotes a slow, gradual process of healing. We cannot heal if we do not slow down or even stop altogether.

Yes, it's uncomfortable being in liminal space, but that's where grief takes you. Without grief, you wouldn't go there. But it is only in liminal space that you can reconstruct your shattered worldview and reemerge as the transformed you that is ready to live and love fully again.

THE UNDERWORLD OF YOUR GRIEF

Most of us know we harbor darkness inside of us. We secretly feel not only pain and fear but also hate, cruelty, lust, and other emotions we judge as shameful. We have thought and done things that we hope no one else ever learns of. Often parts of our grief, too, inhabit this world of shameful, hidden thoughts and feelings.

In Greek mythology, Persephone becomes the queen of the underworld. It is not a throne she sought after, however. Living happily on earth with her family, she is kidnapped by the god of the underworld, Hades, and, after some trickery and back-and-forth, is forced to remain there with him six months of every year. From then on, Persephone embodies the duality of winter/summer, evil/good, darkness/light.

"Your life exactly as it is contains just what is needed for your own journey of healing through the dark emotions. It starts with learning to listen to your heart."

— Miriam Greenspan

"Everything is gestation and then bringing forth."

— Rainer Maria Rilke

All of us are Persephones, really. The trick is in awakening ourselves to the reality that our underworlds are not shameful. Rather, they are simply pieces of the complex puzzle called being human. Like our so-called dark emotions, our grief underworlds cry out for expression. Sharing with others the parts of ourselves that we've so carefully hidden normalizes them. You are not the only one to have felt anger at—or even hatred for—someone who died. You are not the only one, in a moment of emotionality, to have lashed out at someone who didn't deserve it. You are not the only one to have felt relief intermingled with your sadness.

Embrace the underworld of your grief first by visiting it where it lives, in the darkness, then by bringing it with you into the light. Acknowledge it, befriend it, express it. These three actions will reveal it to be a normal and necessary part of your journey. If in sharing your underworld with others you discover parts of yourself that you would like to change, then you can begin working on your personal growth. You may also well discover darker parts of yourself that, if they do not harm you or others, you will decide to honor and uphold.

THE MUSIC OF THE NIGHT

When we are grieving, insomnia is a common challenge. We may have trouble falling asleep, or we may awake in the middle of the night, unable to fall back asleep. Sleeplessness compounds the natural lethargy of grief, so that the next day we may feel even more fatigued and sluggish.

This can be a vicious cycle. If you're not sleeping, you cannot function, and if you can't function, you can't do the work of mourning. If you're not getting adequate sleep night after night, please see your doctor and get help for your insomnia.

"The breeze at dawn has secrets to tell you.

Don't go back to sleep.

You must ask for what you really want.

Don't go back to sleep."

— Rumi

Yet I think that sometimes insomnia, like our dark emotions, has something to teach us. Wakefulness during the dark hours offers us quieter, more mysterious opportunities for reflection than those we may encounter during the day. The self-help author and spiritual thinker Wayne Dyer has said that if you awake in the wee hours of the morning, you should see it as an invitation to connect to your truest self. "Put your feet on the floor, get out of bed, feel the morning breeze, and listen to your inner thoughts," he writes. "The hours before dawn are when you are close to Source, and a great time of inspiration and creativity."

Of course, I understand that the dark hours can also conjure our darkest fears. When we awake in the middle of the night, we may lie in bed ruminating over what we have lost as well as our fears for the future. Even if someone else is sleeping nearby, we may feel deeply alone.

> "The soul reveals itself in cycles and timeless circles of experience. In your dark night, time may seem to crawl or even stop, giving you an opportunity to connect differently with your past."
>
> — Thomas Moore

If you experience such nighttime despair, try to remember that this is an opportunity to embrace your pain. It is a normal and necessary part of your journey. Consider giving it movement, as Dyer suggests, by getting up and out of bed for a while. Keep the lights off or low and pace as you think. Step outside into the moonlight and breathe the night air. Or try writing down your nighttime thoughts and feelings in a journal. Talking to someone else about your dark feelings is always a good idea, but you may not be able to do so in the middle of the night because others are sleeping. However, you can write a letter, type an email, or participate in an online forum at any time.

In the song "The Music of the Night," from *The Phantom of the Opera*, the disfigured man, Erik, who lives and hides in the dark caverns below the opera house, extols the beauty and virtues of darkness. He says that the darkness sharpens our sensations, stirs our imagination, and invites surrender. Unlike the stark, cold light of day, the darkness of night can be seen as lovely and soulful. Your nights, too, can help you find hope and healing. Trust that they will, then work to make it so.

WALLOWING IN THE DARKNESS

I hope by now you are understanding and agreeing with my main point in Truth Two—that we must spend time in and even befriend the darkness of grief before we can even think about entering the light. We must "sit in our wound." We must, for a time, wallow in our grief.

"Wait a minute...," participants in my workshops sometimes protest. "Are you saying it's really OK for people to wallow in their grief? To feel nothing but sorry for themselves?" Let's discuss that for a minute. One meaning of "wallow" is "to lie or roll in." Hippos instinctively wallow in the mud. Goats instinctively wallow in the dirt and dust. The animals naturally behave in this way because wallowing cools their body temperature and cleans them off. It's refreshing. Conversely, we've come to believe that wallowing in our sorrow is bad for us. I believe that this understanding is a product of our contemporary culture's grief-avoidance. It makes us uncomfortable to see others immersed in their pain, so we have appropriated the term "wallow" to describe emotionality and given it a negative connotation. We have contaminated the idea of wallowing with our backward interpretation of the paradoxes. Because wallowing is *good.* After a significant loss, we instinctively and naturally withdraw and sit in the wound of our grief. If we are being honest with ourselves, saying hello to our grief and befriending the darkness, we lie in our pain. We roll in it. And ultimately, our wallowing refreshes us.

> **"When we allow our feelings into our awareness through wallowing in them, we move close to being our true selves."**
>
> — Tina Gilbertson

So yes, it is really OK—necessary even—for people to wallow in their grief for a time. Self-pity can be seen as a form of self-preservation and self-care. (I prefer the idea of self-empathy over self-pity, however. See the discussion on empathy on pages 69 to 70.) Wallowing happens in liminal space—the time betwixt and between. Like the winding of a spring or the crouch before a leap, it is the necessary pause that gives momentum to the coming forward movement.

But I would be remiss if I did not also point out that some people wallow in their grief without ever finding a way to climb out. They take on the long-term persona of the griever, the victim. They become, in essence and usually unknowingly, masochists to their grief.

The term "complicated grief" means grief that has become stuck or derailed in some way. Chronic grief is one form of complicated grief. In chronic grief, grievers experience acute symptoms of grief (inability to experience pleasure, confusion, difficulty focusing, lethargy) that do not change or soften over time.

> "It occurred to me that grief is like a tunnel. You enter it without a choice because you must get to the other side. The darkness of it plays tricks on you, and sometimes you can even forget where you are or what your purpose is. I believe that people, now and again, get lost or stuck in that tunnel and never find their way out."
>
> — Loretta Nyhan

Have you ever known someone who, in the aftermath of a significant loss, was forever depressed or lifeless? Who cocooned themselves in their loss and never emerged? This is what chronic grief looks like, and what it means is that the chronic griever needs help emerging from the darkness. He is stuck. He cannot see the forest for the trees. He runs the very real risk of dying while he is alive. He may have done a very good job of making friends with the darkness, but now he needs help entering the light. He may be clinically depressed. He almost certainly needs the support of a compassionate therapist who has experience working with people in depression and grief.

If you are appropriately and constructively wallowing in the darkness of your grief, you deserve congratulations. Befriending the darkness of grief takes courage and hard work. But if you find yourself stuck in the darkness, I hope you will muster the courage to get help. Do not be ashamed. You have done nothing wrong. You simply need a helping hand, as we all do at times. Counseling (and sometimes medication) will help you enter the light.

THE LIGHT OF EMPATHY IN THE DARKNESS

The darkness of grief is a necessary experience. It is a natural time of depression, stillness, withdrawal, unsettledness, and pain. It is largely an interior struggle. But even in your time of darkness, you can and should reach out for glimpses of light.

> "When we honestly ask ourselves which people in our lives mean the most to us, we often find it is those who, instead of giving advice, solutions, or cures, have chosen rather to share our pain and touch our wounds with a warm and tender hand."
>
> — Henri Nouwen

We've talked about the difference between grief and mourning. Grief is the internal experience, while mourning is the expression of grief outside yourself. In the darkness of your grief, mourning in the presence of compassionate, empathetic listeners lights a candle of hope.

Talk about your grief. Tell your story of love and loss. Turn to helpers who are good at listening without judging, being present to others in pain, and capable of bearing witness without trying to "solve your problem." Most of all, seek out people who are truly empathetic, not just sympathetic.

> *"Empathy is an act of imagination—to participate with another person in her life is to make a connection not possible in the night of despair."*
>
> — John Tarrant

When people are sympathetic to you, they are noticing and feeling concern for your circumstances, usually at a distance. They are "feeling sorry" for you. They are feeling "pity" for you. They are looking at your situation from the outside, and they are acknowledging your distress passively. They may be offering a simple solution, platitude, or distraction. Sometimes sympathy also includes a touch (or a heavy dose) of judgment or superiority. Sympathy is "feeling for" someone else.

Empathy, on the other hand, is about making an emotional connection. It is a more active process—one in which the listener tries to understand and feel your experience from the inside out. The listener is not judging you or your thoughts and feelings. She is not offering simple solutions. Instead, she is making herself vulnerable to your thoughts, feelings, and circumstances by looking for connections to similar thoughts, feelings, and circumstances inside her. She is being present and allowing herself to be taught by you. Empathy is "feeling with" someone else.

In your time of darkness, the loyal empathy of just one other human being can be the candle you need to find your way through to healing.

THE LIGHT OF LEVITY AND HUMOR IN THE DARKNESS

While you are making friends with the darkness of your grief, the glow of empathy can help you survive. Likewise, sparks of levity and humor are essential in the darkness.

I've said that you must dose yourself with your pain and dark emotions, because you cannot feel them all at once, in one grand grieving session. Grief doesn't work like that—in part because grief takes time (forever, actually), in part because grief's full force would kill you if taken in too large a portion. In between your normal and necessary moments of befriending your pain, you must also befriend laughter and love.

"What soap is to the body, laughter is to the soul."

— Yiddish proverb

You've probably heard the term "dark comedy." Also called "black comedy," dark comedy is humor that makes fun of subjects that we normally consider taboo. "Gallows humor" is another synonym, as is "morbid sense of humor." Dark comedy is a form of befriending the darkness because it brings the darkness into the light. In darkly comic movies and plays, characters display their dark sides for laughs. What we're laughing at in the Billy Crystal and Danny Devito movie *Throw Momma From the Train*, for example, are the frank, out-in-the-open discussions of the two men as they make goofball plans to bump off the curmudgeonly mother.

My point isn't that you should watch or enjoy dark comedies, necessarily. My point is that the existence of dark comedies is evidence of our need to bring our darkest thoughts and feelings out of the closet and in doing so, befriend them. If we can find the humor in them sometimes, then all the better.

By all means, look for ways to dose yourself with levity and laughter as you journey in the darkness. Reach out to connect with others you love, as well. Levity, laughter, and love are like sparklers in the blackness of an evening's Fourth of July celebrations. They distract and delight, if only for a moment or two. They remind us of the goodness of life. And they give us hope that even as we grieve, our futures hold the promise of more sparkly magic.

ENTERING THE LIGHT

Truth Two says that you must make friends with the darkness before you can enter the light. But what is the light? There really is no set destination on the journey through grief. The light of healing in grief is not exactly like the light at the end of a tunnel. Reconciliation, which we've already reviewed, is the goal, but it is not a fixed end point or perfect state of bliss. At least here on Earth, bittersweet is as sweet as it gets.

> *"When life is sweet, say thank you and celebrate. And when life is bitter, say thank you and grow."*
>
> — Shauna Niequist

As with the process of saying hello and goodbye after a loss, the process of making friends with the darkness and entering the light is not a lockstep, always-forward-moving journey. Instead, we experience flickers of light in the darkness as well as washes of darkness during our days in the light. Life is always, in every moment, a blend of joy and despair, contentment and anxiety, love and loss.

The Chinese yin-yang symbol represents the duality of many experiences in life. The shape of the symbol is a perfect circle—in other words, a unified whole. But comprising the circle are two comma shapes—one black (the yin) and one white (the yang). And within each comma shape is a dot of the opposite color.

The symbol is a visual reminder that everything is comprised of both darkness and light. Yet the darkness and the light are not opposing forces. Rather, they are complementary twins that only together form a whole. What's more, the drop of white in the black yin and the drop of black in the white yang remind us that nothing is purely dark or light, good or bad. Instead, life is made up of people, places, actions, things, and experiences that are mixtures of both.

And so, think of the light as the thoughts and feelings you want to experience more of. Hope. Gratitude. Happiness. Joy. Love. Peace. The more you make friends with the darkness, the more your capacity for these thoughts and feelings will grow.

"My desire to live is as intense as ever, and though my heart is broken, hearts are made to be broken: that is why God sends sorrow into the world... To me, suffering seems now a sacramental thing that makes those whom it touches holy."

— Oscar Wilde

TRUTH THREE:

YOU MUST GO
BACKWARD BEFORE YOU
CAN GO FORWARD.

"Life must be lived forwards,
but it can be understood
only backwards."

— Soren Kierkegaard

SINCE YOUR LOSS, WELL-MEANING BUT MISINFORMED FRIENDS AND FAMILY MEMBERS have probably been telling you some version of

"He/she would want you to keep living your life."

"Time heals all wounds."

"Just keep putting one foot in front of the other."

"You need to put the past in the past."

Or, as my mother was repeatedly told when my father died four months after their golden wedding anniversary, "You had him for 50 years." Not only do these oft-offered clichés diminish your significant and unique loss, they imply that moving forward—in your life and in time—is what will ease your suffering. The truth is, paradoxically, in grief you have to go backward before you can go forward.

Grief is by its very nature a recursive process. That means it curves and spirals back on itself. It is repetitive. It covers the same ground more than once. In fact, it *requires* repetition to eventually soften and become reconciled.

Our cultural misconception about moving forward in grief stems in part from the concept of the "stages of grief," popularized in 1969 by Elisabeth Kubler-Ross's landmark text, *On Death and Dying*. In this important book, Dr. Kubler-Ross lists the five stages of grief that she saw terminally ill patients experience in the face of their own impending deaths: denial, anger, bargaining, depression, and acceptance. However, she never intended for her five stages to be interpreted as a rigid, linear sequence to be followed by all mourners.

Grief is not a train track toward acceptance. Instead, it is more of a "getting lost in the woods" and almost always gives rise to a mixture of many thoughts and feelings at once. A feeling that predominates at any given time, anger, say, may dissipate for a while but then later return full force. Grief is not even a two steps forward, one step backward kind of journey—it is often a one step forward, two steps in a circle, one step backward process. It takes time, patience, and, yes, lots of backward motion before forward motion predominates.

"The common wisdom about getting on with life can backfire, because the only way to move ahead is not to deny or repress the past. Escaping the past makes you a slave to it; you are not free to be freely in the present."

— Thomas Moore

In Greek mythology, the phoenix is a bird that periodically dies and is reborn. But before it can be reborn, it first spontaneously burns itself to ashes. In other words, it starts over. As you are grieving, think of the phoenix as you embark on your necessary backward journey.

"If you seek a spark, you will find it in the ashes."

— Elie Wiesel

GOING BACKWARD THROUGH RITUAL

It seems that humankind has always instinctively understood the need for ritual at times of significant transitions. We have already talked a little about the important role of the funeral ceremony to carry us meaningfully through the transition of a death, but backward-looking rituals for other reasons are also myriad.

In the centuries from 250 to 900, for example, the Mayans intentionally burned their houses to the ground every 40 or 50 years, on important dates corresponding with the Mayan calendar. They tore down the walls, shattered their sacred crockery, and sometimes placed the body of a dead loved one atop the pyre, setting the whole thing on fire. Then they built a new home on top of all the remains. In these de-animation and reanimation rituals, the Mayans routinely and ritualistically honored the past—and even physically incorporated the past into their futures.

"The soul is inclined toward the past rather than the future... In outer life, we may leave a person or a place, but in memory and dreams the soul clings to these former attachments."

— Thomas Moore

Native Americans also ritually looked to their ancestors for wisdom and guidance. Their shamans, or spiritual leaders, put themselves into trances to communicate with the spirits of the dead, who would pass along advice to help heal the sick or make decisions of importance to the tribe. (In fact, the word shaman means "to see in the dark.")

Still to this day, coming-of-age ceremonies in cultures all around the world require young people to follow ancient traditions and look to the history of their communities to prepare them to enter adulthood. In Malaysia, for example, 11-year-old girls prepare for the celebration called Khatam Al Koran by memorizing the last chapter of the Koran, which they then recite aloud together in a public ceremony.

Days of the Dead celebrations in various cultures are another example of ritual looking backward. Once a year, people in

Mexico—where *Día de los Muertos* is a public holiday—actively remember and celebrate those who have died. Shrines, gifts, and food for the dead are placed to entice their souls to visit. All Saints Day and All Souls Day rituals are a Christian equivalent.

Throughout history, when the import of an event or transition in our lives is more profound than everyday words and actions can capture, we have had the wisdom to turn to ritual. And in our rituals, we often looked backward first—to our ancestors, to our holy or touchstone texts, to our traditions—before we celebrated what would come next.

"This is what rituals are for. We do spiritual ceremonies as human beings in order to create a safe resting place for our most complicated feelings of joy or trauma, so that we don't have to haul those feelings around with us forever, weighing us down. We all need such places of ritual safekeeping."

— Elizabeth Gilbert

Yet in contemporary times, as we pare down and even abandon more and more of the rituals that have long imbued our lives with meaning and purpose, we seem to be forgetting the need to go backward before going forward during rites of passage—including the death of a loved one.

Here and there, though, backward-looking rituals persist. In New York City, a stream of police cars pulls up to the 9/11 terrorist-disaster site early every morning. They flash their emergency lights but do not turn on their sirens. The police officers park, get out of their cars, and stand shoulder to shoulder in silence for a moment before returning to their vehicles and beginning their day of public service. What the officers seem to subconsciously understand is that this simple, quiet, backward-looking mourning ritual grounds their presents and their futures. When it comes to grief and mourning, we would all be well served to resurrect old rituals, sustain existing rituals, and create new rituals that honor the natural and necessary need to look backward before going forward.

GOING BACKWARD THROUGH MEMORY

Do you remember the man we met in Truth One—the husband who was saying goodbye to his dying wife? After her death, do you imagine him driving back to the home they shared for many years and immediately packing up his wife's belongings, opening an account on a dating website, and starting to plan his next vacation?

> "We must listen to the music of the past to sing in the present and dance into the future."
>
> — Alan D. Wolfelt, Ph.D.

Of course you don't! These activities—all of which could be seen as signs of "moving forward"—are ridiculous in the immediate aftermath of significant loss. What is the man likely to do instead? He may take her photo down from the mantel and gaze at it. He might wrap her scarf around his neck and bury his nose in its folds, inhaling her scent. He might sit and close his eyes in an effort to conjure her face, her voice, her smile.

No, our new widower is most certainly NOT moving forward. What is he instinctively and necessarily doing instead? He is going backward, returning to his memories of his precious wife.

And yet when we talk to each other about loss and grief, we often perpetuate the falsehood that we need always to be moving ahead.

I recently counseled a widower. Eight weeks after his wife's death, his friends told him, "It's time for you to move on." He came to see me because he just couldn't reconcile what he was feeling inside with his friends' advice. Needless to say, I affirmed his instinctive need to go backward before going forward. A 44-year-old woman I counseled had a similar experience. This time, just three days (!!!) after her relatively young husband died, a group of women in her neighborhood came to her and said, "We've been talking about you. You're still fairly good looking. We're going to put you on Match.com."

"Death ends a life, not a relationship."

— Mitch Albom

Oh, the hubris and folly of thinking we can move forward before going backward. For the survivors, the loss created by death is the loss of the physical presence of the person who died. In the physical plane, your relationship with the person has ended. And so you grieve. But on the emotional and spiritual planes, your relationship with the person who died continues *because you will always have a relationship of memory.* Precious memories, dreams reflecting the significance of the relationship, and objects that link you to the person who died are examples of some of the things that give testimony to a different form of a continued relationship.

"The word 'remembering' implicitly conveys a second meaning—re-membering, putting back together something that has been sundered, broken apart."

— Ernest Kurtz

And so you must look backward through the lens of memory. Embracing your memories is indeed instinctive, but also it is often a very slow and, at times, painful process that occurs in small steps. Remember—don't try to do all of your work of mourning at once. Go slowly and be patient with yourself.

If you were fortunate enough to have had a meaningful funeral experience after your loss, you probably realized that the funeral helps us go backward through memory. Several of my childhood friends came to the visitation for my father's funeral. "We loved your dad," they told me. "He was the only adult in the neighborhood who let us play in the street. He always said, 'The cars will stop. Go out for a pass.'" As they and other guests spoke to me and shared their memories of my father, I was privileged to revisit special moments I had forgotten and sometimes never knew about. The eulogy and the reception after the funeral are also rich in memory sharing and the healing backward gaze.

But the funeral isn't the only opportunity to remember. Following are a few example of mourning actions you can take to go backward through memory while simultaneously embracing the reality that the person has died:

- Talking out or writing out favorite memories

- Giving yourself permission to keep some special keepsakes or "linking objects"
- Displaying photos of the person who died
- Visiting places of special significance that stimulate memories of times shared together
- Reviewing photo albums at special times such as holidays, birthdays, and anniversaries

Because our society is forgetting the need to go backward before going forward, your work to honestly and openly remember in these ways may be condemned. If others imply or outright tell you that focusing on memories, photos, and belongings of the person who died is wrong, don't believe them. Try to understand that their thinking has been skewed by our grief-avoiding contemporary culture.

> "You can't connect the dots looking forward. You can only connect them looking backward. This approach has never let me down, and it has made all the difference in my life."
>
> — Steve Jobs

In my experience, remembering the past is the very thing that eventually makes hoping for the future possible. Your life will open to renewed hope, love, and joy only to the extent that you first embrace the past. Those who fail to go backward before marching forward after a loss often find themselves stuck in the morass of carried grief. (See page 97.)

GOING BACKWARD AS GRIEVING CHILDREN DO

Children who are grieving have much to teach us about the necessity of going backward before we can go forward in the aftermath of a significant loss. In fact, children, who have not yet been contaminated by our harmful cultural "rules" around grief and loss, are in fact our most organic, instinctive teachers.

After someone they love dies, children often start to display what often gets referred to as "regressive behaviors." They may revive old, outgrown habits, such as talking baby talk or throwing tantrums. They may start to wet the bed again and often become more clingy to their parents or primary caregivers. Older children may start to suck their thumbs again or suddenly seem unable to tie their own shoes, even though they've been doing it themselves for years.

What these children unconsciously are doing is going backward to a time in their lives that they felt safe. They are also, in essence, asking to be taken care of. That is why I prefer to call them "care-eliciting behaviors" instead of regressive behaviors. "I need to know I am still loved and you will still take care of me!" they are saying behaviorally.

Unfortunately, in our mourning-avoidant culture, which doesn't understand or foster the instinctive need to go backward before going forward, grieving children who exhibit regressive behaviors are often shamed by adults. Sadly, they are often "forgotten mourners" in a culture that attempts to keep going forward out of lack of understanding of this paradox.

GOING BACKWARD TO YOUR BEGINNINGS

The person you are today is the sum total of all the experiences that have touched your life. While your genetics also come into play, all the things that happen to you and all the people you interact with shape you. And because time is linear, your core is shaped in your earliest years—in childhood.

> **"But why had he always felt so strongly the magnetic pull of home, why had he thought so much about it and remembered it with such blazing accuracy, if it did not matter, and if this little town, and the immortal hills around it, was not the only home he had on earth? He did not know. All that he knew was that the years flow by like water, and that one day men come home again."**
>
> — Thomas Wolfe

We're kind of like snowmen and snowwomen. As babies, we are snowballs, which then begin to roll across the landscape of our lives. We pick up more and more snow as we go. We grow and change. But deep inside of us, at our center, is always that first snowball, packed by the hands of our parents or other caretakers.

The rock star Sting learned this in middle age, when he found himself creatively stuck. This was unusual for him. He had always been a prolific songwriter, but try as he might, he could not come up with any new material. This period of writer's block went on for frustrating year after frustrating year...until he decided to go home.

You see, Sting grew up in England "in the shadow of a shipyard." His family and his community were poor, but what little money and pride they did have came from their labors in the noisy and dangerous shipyard that was the centerpiece of their town. At the age of eight, Sting—who at that time was known by his birth name of Gordon Summer—was given a battered old guitar. Soon he came to see that guitar as his ticket out of the shipyard, out of the clutches of that small, impoverished community.

"We leave something of ourselves behind when we leave a place. We stay there, even though we go away. And there are things in us that we can find again only by going back there."

— Pascal Mercier

Sting's dreams carried him far and away for many years—until the day he found himself stopped in his tracks. After long years of creative drought, he finally realized that looking backward was the way to go forward again. He turned an empathetic eye and heart to the people and stories of his childhood, and new songs began to pour out of him, practically writing themselves. *The Last Ship*, released in 2013, was his first full-length album since his 2003 album *Sacred Love*.

What Sting grew to understand was that his story did not begin after he left the shipyard. It began on the day he was born. And his formative years, as they are for all of us, were an integral, inextricable part of his story. Actually, Sting's story began before he was born, because the worldview and customs of his community had been developing for centuries before he came along.

As you proactively work to feel and express your grief, you might also be well served to "go home again." Go backward to your childhood, to the place, as John Denver sang in "Take Me Home,

Country Roads," you belong. Think about the people and places you loved. Remember the things that you were most passionate about. Then go back even further and consider the cultural or ethnic heritage that shaped you.

Reflect on your past. The word "reflect" comes from the Latin words *re,* meaning "back," and *flectere,* meaning "to bend." When you reflect on your past, you bend backward. You turn your gaze to that which is behind you—because it is not actually behind you, it is still a part of you.

"The beginning is never the beginning. In order to move forward, there must first be an ending. Otherwise we merely accumulate emotional baggage and carry our burdens from one situation to another. Perhaps a lot of our struggle to get past what we'll never get over is that we try to get a fresh start before we put an end to the past."

— John F. Westfall

Consider, too, the ways in which your family of origin handled loss, grief, and mourning. Were there open, loving discussions about death and loss? Did your parents mourn openly and support you in your need to mourn? If not, what were the "rules," spoken or unspoken, about emotions and their expression in your household? And how did your parents' cultural and ethnic backgrounds contribute to these rules?

Also remind yourself of the rituals that have, over the years, comforted you and given your life meaning. What has helped you cope with stress and loss in the past? Make a list of the most difficult times in your life and the ways in which you helped yourself live through them. Did you spend time with family? Write? Turn to your faith? Help take care of someone else? Which activities calm you? Getting a massage, taking a walk, going for a swim, talking to your sister on the phone, walking the dog, reading a book, meditating? These are the survival techniques that can also help you today and every day.

Make note of any of these that are unhealthy ways of trying to avoid your suffering, as well, such as substance abuse, gambling, overspending, overeating, or premature replacement of a relationship, for example. We want to be sure these are not the coping skills you turn to during this difficult time. For most of us, it takes the routine use of a new coping skill over several months to replace any old habits or strategies that are detrimental.

"A man travels the world
over in search of what he needs
and returns home to find it."

— George Moore

In his book *The Act of Creation,* author Arthur Koestler referred to psychotherapy as *reculer pour mieux sauter*—French for, roughly, "going backward to be able to leap forward better." The process of going backward to your beginnings, whether you do it on your own, in a support group, or with the help of a compassionate counselor, can in effect give you a running start when you turn around to go forward again.

The dying instinctively know this. As noted gerontologist Robert Butler pointed out, people who know they are dying almost always go backward to their earliest memories. They naturally reminisce and conduct a kind of life review. In grief, our instinct is the same.

At times of significant loss or, as in Sting's case, periods of feeling stuck and unproductive, you will almost certainly find that going backward is an essential step on the road to going forward. On your journey home, you may also encounter old griefs that also need exploring. We'll take more about those on page 97.

GOING BACKWARD TO TELL YOUR STORY

A vital part of mourning is often "telling the story" over and over again. And the story of your love and loss is a backward-looking process.

> *"Recounting of a life story... leads one inevitably to the consideration of problems which are no longer psychological, but spiritual."*
>
> — Paul Tournier

You might find yourself telling the story of the death. You might find yourself telling the story of the relationship. You might find yourself wanting to talk about particular parts of the story more than others. Do you keep thinking about a certain moment or time period? If so, this means you should share this part of the story with others.

What if you don't want to talk about your loss? It's OK to respect this feeling for a while, but soon you'll need to start talking about it or find other ways to express it. Keeping your thoughts and feelings about the death inside you only makes them more powerful. Giving them voice allows them to soften.

Find people who are willing to listen to you tell your story, over and over again if necessary, without judgment. These are often "fellow strugglers" who have had similar losses. But remember that not everyone will be able to be a compassionate listener. While you may wish everyone you know could be a support to you, keep in mind my "rule of thirds." One third of people are usually neutral: they don't help you or hurt you. One third are harmful and end up making you feel worse than you did before you were in their presence. And one third will be your empathetic, hope-filled companions. Seek out your friends and family who are in this latter group. Look for listeners who can be present to your pain without trying to diminish it, "solve" it, or take it away.

"Through storytelling we can come to know who we are in new and unforeseen ways. We can also reveal to others what is deepest in our hearts, in the process, building bridges. The very act of sharing a story with another human being contradicts the extreme isolation that characterizes so many of our lives. And, because stories take time and patience, they serve as potent antidotes to a modern society's preoccupation with technology and speed."

— Richard Stone

Because stories of love and loss take time, patience, and unconditional love, they serve as powerful antidotes to a modern society that is all too often preoccupied with getting you to go forward. Whether you share your story with a friend, a family member, a coworker, or a fellow traveler in grief whom you've met through a support group, having others bear witness to the telling of your unique story is one way to go backward on the pathway to eventually going forward.

"The practice of telling stories does in some way 'heal'—make whole. Perhaps the most important task of stories is the healing of identity, the making whole that comes by connecting our present with our memory."

— Ernest Kurtz

GOING BACKWARD TO HEAL OLD GRIEFS

After a loss, when you say hello before saying goodbye, make friends with the darkness before entering the light, and go backward before trying to go forward—in other words, when you are honest and open about your loss and work to actively mourn—you create movement. Another way to say this is that mourning puts your emotions in motion.

I use the term "perturbation" to refer to this capacity to experience change and movement. To integrate grief, you must be touched by what you experience *and* you must express what you experience. If you do not allow yourself to be touched, on the other hand, and/or if you do not express what is touching you on the inside, you can't be changed by it. Instead, you may well become "stuck."

So, if you are grieving but not mourning, if you are not honoring

FINDING A GRIEF COMPANION

A number of years ago I realized that therapists needed a new model for caring for clients experiencing grief. Client-centered talk therapy served as a good foundation, but truly effective grief counselors thought of grief in a more holistic and spiritual way. They did not see grief as a disorder or a disease but rather as a natural and necessary process. They also did not try to "cure" their clients' grief; rather, they saw themselves as companions on the journey. And they understood and promulgated the three Truths of the paradoxes of mourning.

Since that time, I have trained hundreds of lay and professional grief caregivers in this philosophy. To find one near you, I invite you to call the Center for Loss at (970) 226-6050. If you are interested in seeking the support of a grief counselor, we will do our best to refer you to a caregiver who will deeply understand and honor your journey through grief. The Association of Death Education and Counseling (www.adec.org) is another good resource. On their website is a tool that will help you find a certified bereavement care specialist near you.

Once you have found a grief counselor, I hope you will also consider whether or not she is a good match for you. My book *Understanding Your Grief* contains a section called "Reaching Out to a Grief Counselor" (pp. 166-169). It's important to work with a counselor whom you trust and like.

the forgotten Truths, you are doing what I call "carrying" your grief. That is, you are carrying it inside you, and you will continue to carry it until you express it.

When you carry your pain instead of mourning it, it will come back to haunt you. It will keep trying to get your attention until you give it the attention it demands and deserves. As Michel de Montaigne once observed, "The man who fears suffering is already suffering from what he fears."

"Pain insists upon being attended to. God whispers to us in our pleasures, speaks in our consciences, but shouts in our pains. It is his megaphone to rouse a deaf world."

— C.S. Lewis

Pain that is left unhealed and unfinished business that is never explored may well destroy your enthusiasm for life and living. Unhealed pain has the potential of extinguishing your divine spark—that which gives your life meaning and purpose. Unhealed pain can deny you your creativity, your gifts, and your talents. The result is that these parts of yourself go stagnant or unclaimed inside of you, wishing they could get out but feeling trapped.

"To come to terms with our feelings is to be vulnerable to the arrows of the past still flying through the skies of the present."

— David Richo

What's more, carried grief compounds. Consider that the pain you are experiencing today may be the result of not only your most recent loss but all the unmourned losses from earlier in your life. My experience as a grief counselor and educator tells me that carried grief is often a significant contributor to ongoing problems with trust, depression, and anxiety.

At right are some of the common symptoms I have observed in people who carry the unmourned pain of old griefs.

On a societal level, I believe carried grief is the source of most of our world conflicts. Cultures and countries fight with one another over unhealed grief and disagreements from hundreds and even thousands of years ago. What if we could recognize this and mourn instead of fight?

Going backward to uncover any old griefs that you may be carrying and then working to mourn them is at the heart of your healing. Healing carried pain will not "just happen." It will require you to identify, befriend, and mourn your carried pain.

SYMPTOMS OF CARRIED GRIEF

Difficulties with trust and intimacy

Depression and negative outlook

Anxiety and panic attacks

Psychic numbing and disconnection

Irritability and agitation

Substance abuse, addictions, eating disorders

Chronic fatigue

Physical problems, real or imagined

I have had the honor of working with hundreds of people who have allowed me to support them in mourning carried pain. I use the term "catch-up mourning" to describe the process that helps them work through their carried grief and eventually experience a more on-purpose, joyful life.

If you mourn your carried pain, you can truly live until you die. In the broadest sense, deciding to address your carried pain is a choice between opposites: a life devoid of deep feeling or a deeply felt life; escapist activities or meaningful activities. It means choosing between experiencing a life with its very real pains and pleasures or living in an anesthetized fog in which authentic feelings are inhibited; between a consciousness of our deepest feelings, or a vague, muted self-awareness.

CATCH-UP MOURNING

Going backward and giving attention to any grief you have carried from past losses in your life. The purpose of going back and doing your grief work is anchored in eventually freeing you to go forward with newfound meaning and purpose in your life, living, and loving.

As I've said, our mourning-avoidant culture often invites you to go forward. So if you find that you are carrying grief, do not shame yourself. You may have learned early in life to deny feelings of loss and to wear a mask, and eventually you lost contact with your inner self. Significant adults in your childhood may have encouraged you to disown fear, grief, anger, and pain, because such feelings made them uncomfortable. Adults who carry grief tend to raise children who carry grief, not only through direct communication but through their own behavior, which proclaims to the child what is appropriate, proper, and acceptable. And if even your family of origin was good at embracing pain and supporting one another in grief, your culture and community likely was not.

So how do you heal any old griefs you might be carrying? How do you go backward and "do" catch-up mourning? The catch-up mourning process is outside the scope of this book on the paradoxes of mourning, but if you are interested in learning more about it, I invite you to read my book *Living in the Shadow of the Ghosts of Grief.* Rest assured that not only can it be done, it is an extremely empowering and effective backward-looking process that can help you go on to move forward in ways you never thought possible.

GOING BACKWARD TO NAME YOUR GRATITUDE

Even if in going backward you discover that you are carrying old griefs that need your attention, I don't want you to misunderstand that the process of going backward is all about digging up and working through the "bad" stuff. In remembering, returning to your beginnings, and re-storying your life, you will also find many people and experiences to be thankful for.

Studies have shown that the process of writing down what you are grateful for is a practice that creates lasting, positive change. Consider starting a gratitude journal. In your work going backward, take time to write down thoughts and memories for which you are grateful.

> "Those who have gone 'down' are the only ones who understand 'up.'"
>
> — Richard Rohr

Which relationships in your life are you most grateful for and why? Write about them. Or if you'd rather, tell the story of those relationships to someone who cares about you. And most important of all, express your gratitude directly to those people. If they are still alive, write them personal and detailed letters of thanks. Or take them out to lunch or dinner for the express purpose of telling them how much they mean to you and thanking them. Even for the special people in your life who have passed on, it is not too late to express your gratitude. Write them letters and read them aloud at their gravesites. Or go somewhere that reminds you strongly of them and speak out loud to them. Who knows? Maybe they can hear you. And no matter what, the recognition and expression of your gratitude will help *you*.

> "Acknowledging the good that you already have in your life is the foundation for all abundance."
>
> — Eckhart Tolle

When you fill your life with gratitude, you invoke a self-fulfilling prophecy: what you pay attention to will be magnified and repeated. Reflect on the moments of joy and love each day. Honor them and have gratitude for them. Be grateful for your physical health and your beautiful spirit. Be grateful for your family and friends and the concern of strangers. Above all, be grateful for this very moment. When you are grateful, you train your brain to look for the good in life, and you prepare the way for inner peace.

GOING BACKWARD TO BEGIN ANEW

You know how in board games you sometimes land on an unfortunate square that sends you all the way back to the beginning? The death of someone you love can be like that. It can—indeed, it usually needs to—send you backward in all of the ways we've been talking about in Truth Three.

When you go backward through ritual and memory, when you go backward to your beginnings, to re-story your life and to heal old griefs, you are doing a kind of starting over. You are pressing the reset button. That makes now a good time to reassess your priorities and reconsider how you want to spend the rest of your precious life.

> **"People may spend their whole lives climbing the ladder of success only to find, once they reach the top, that the ladder is leaning against the wrong wall."**
>
> —Thomas Merton

You've witnessed a life come to an end. Was it a rich, satisfying life? What can you learn from it? What gives *your* life meaning? What doesn't? Take steps to spend more of your time on the former and less on the latter.

Now may be the time to reconfigure your life. Choose a satisfying new career. Go back to school. Begin volunteering. Move closer to your family. Be kinder and more compassionate. The key is to go backward and dig deep to uncover your true passions—whatever they may be—and your true self. Then, move forward to manifest them.

GOING FORWARD IN GRIEF

I hope you are beginning to understand the necessity of going backward in grief before you can go forward. But as we've also explored, the going-forward nature of grief is itself a paradox. "Progress" in grief is difficult to pinpoint. Grief is something we never truly get over. Instead, it is an ongoing, recursive process that unfolds over many, many months and years.

Something you *can* hold onto after you have put time and energy into your backward grief work, though, is hope. Hope is an expectation of a good that is yet to be. Hope is about the future. Going forward in grief means, in part, fostering hope.

How do you foster hope? You can write down your intentions for the future. You can make plans with friends and family so that you always have things to look forward to. You can craft a vision board—a piece of poster board covered with photos and images that capture what you want your future to be like. You can make goals and achieve them. Start with small, easy goals that are only a few days out, then work toward longer-term goals.

"You don't have to have it all figured out to move forward."

— Unknown

And remember, as long as you are doing the work of grief—actively expressing your grief and living the Truths—you are going forward in grief, even though it may not always feel that way. You may not notice that you are going forward as it is happening, but one day you will look up and find that you have indeed moved and changed.

"Never doubt that a small group of thoughtful, committed citizens can change the world. Indeed, it is the only thing that ever has."

— Margaret Mead

A FINAL WORD

I SPEND MANY WEEKS EACH YEAR TRAVELING the United States and Canada (and sometimes the globe) to give presentations on the principles of grief and mourning. Teaching is my passion. It's my mission to help people mourn well so that they can go on to live and love well.

I've found that whenever I mention the three paradoxes of mourning we've explored in this book, my audience nods and leans in. They are captivated by the notion of forgotten Truths. And when I explain what the Truths are—hello/goodbye; darkness/light; backward/forward—my listeners seem immediately to "get it." It's as if I'm telling them something they've known all along but needed a reminder of. Actually, it's as if they've been hypnotized, but I've snapped my fingers and they've awoken.

We as human beings understand and appreciate the three paradoxes of mourning because *the Truths are built into our DNA*. They are natural and instinctive. But sometimes in the course of human history, new paradigms arise, bringing us progress but also sometimes obliterating what was good and right about the old ways of doing things.

Starting in the 1800s, the rise of the industrial age followed in quick succession by the dawning of the information age brought us many fantastic developments. Medical progress has doubled our lifespans. Computers have enabled global economies and awareness, among untold other miracles. In all facets of human life, the transformation in the past 200 years has been truly mind-boggling.

> *"It has become appallingly obvious that our technology has exceeded our humanity."*
>
> — Albert Einstein

There is much to be celebrated in our progress. But along the way, we also forgot to hold onto much of our hard-won, ancient wisdom about loss, grief, and healing.

In recent years I've been noticing that in other life arenas, movements are underway to restore many of the good things that were waylaid during our dizzying decades of progress. The slow food movement, for example, seeks to expose the hazards of globally sourced foods, restore our connection to how and where our food is grown, and resurrect the sustainable, healthy, and community-enhancing farm-to-table practices of days gone by.

In urban design, we are looking to the past at community-building principles like walkability, human scale, front porches, and public gathering spaces. The goal now is to create new cities that incorporate modern technology as well as the livability of old cities.

And in retail, big box stores may be going the way of the dodo. We are reconsidering our habits of shopping at discount stores and online for cheap, generic goods. Instead, we are increasingly spending our money on local, artisanal products that are not only more beautiful and interesting but also better support the communities in which we live.

Similarly, the time is right, I believe, to get behind what I'm coining the Slow Grief movement.

> *"The power to question is the basis of all human progress."*
>
> — Indira Gandhi

The Slow Grief movement acknowledges that loss is as much a part of the human experience as love. It recognizes that loss changes us forever and that grief is a normal, necessary, and, yes, *sssllloooww* process. It also proclaims the need for people to express their grief and to be supported by their communities. And it asks us to look to the past to recapture the healing wisdom and customs we have almost lost.

In the Slow Food movement, many elementary schools are planting edible gardens to teach children where food comes from and what actual food looks and tastes like. In the Slow Grief movement, perhaps we can incorporate simple rituals and sacred spaces into elementary schools that help young children explore their natural instincts to be open and honest about all feelings, including the so-called dark emotions of loss.

In the same vein, in our efforts to rein in medical costs and champion the wellness model over the sickness model that has predominated for a number of decades now, we are re-examining when and how best to use, judiciously, prescription drugs, diagnostic procedures, and surgeries. In the Slow Grief movement, it's time to remove grief from the purview of medicine altogether.

Let's strike it from the list of illnesses and take it back as a normal, natural, and necessary spiritual process that in fact fosters wellness.

Progressives believe that education is the key to solving the world's most intransigent problems, like poverty, hunger, and violence. I don't disagree, but I would add that emotional and spiritual education and support is equally foundational. The Slow Grief movement understands that loss is love's conjoined twin, and that loss is, inevitably, a bracingly large component of the human condition. Therefore, until such time as our culture is grief-embracing—and grief openness and support is built into every family, group, and organization—the principles of grief and mourning as well as the skill of empathy must be taught overtly in schools and corporations, much as anti-bullying awareness is taught today.

Just as in the Slow Food movement we take the time to prepare real food and share it with those we care about, in the Slow Grief movement we would take the time to listen to one another without judging and encourage the sharing of internal thoughts and feelings, no matter what they are.

After all, if you agree that grief, when fully and openly explored, expressed, and supported, is a transformative experience, you'll probably also agree that this transformation could be harnessed for good. If we helped people in our communities mourn more fully, wouldn't we also be helping them to go on to love more fully? And if we helped them love more fully, wouldn't we quickly be bettering the very fabric of our society?

And in opposition to the international big box store chains, the artisan movement champions local "makers" who sew clothing, cobble shoes, and craft all manner of goods and art. In the Slow

Grief movement, I hope we recognize the art of the compassionate grief companion—the professional or trained lay caregiver who creates safe places for those in grief to mourn fully and honestly. The contemporary therapies that are so popular today, billed as "solution-oriented" and "cognitive-behavioral"-based, are all about speed, efficiency, and cognition. They attempt to rid people of their grief symptoms as quickly as possible. The Slow Grief movement supports caregiving that is as slow as the mourner needs it to be as well as heart-based.

I hope you'll join me in the Slow Grief movement. Think about what you can do in your organization and community to enhance grief awareness and support. As has been the case with all other human rights causes throughout history, the Slow Grief movement will likely seem radical in its early days. Don't let that put you off. Stand up for what's right. Reach out to others whose lives have been changed by loss and ask them to help. As Gandhi said, be the change you wish to see in the world.

"Every great dream begins with a dreamer. Always remember, you have within you the strength, the patience, and the passion to reach for the stars to change the world."

— Harriet Tubman

If you'd like to communicate with me about your ideas for fostering the Slow Grief movement in your organization or community, I invite you to email me: DrWolfelt@centerforloss.com.

God bless you. I hope to hear from you.

ABOUT THE AUTHOR

Dr. Alan D. Wolfelt is a respected educator, author, and grief counselor who believes that after a loss, we need to mourn well to go on to live and love well again. He is a responsible rebel who challenges our culture's paradoxical misunderstanding of grief.

Among Dr. Wolfelt's bestselling books on grief are *Understanding Your Grief*, *Healing Your Grieving Heart*, and *Loving from the Outside In, Mourning from the Inside Out*.

Dr. Wolfelt also serves as Director of the Center for Loss and Life Transition in Fort Collins, Colorado, and is on the faculty at the University of Colorado Medical School's Department of Family Medicine.

TRAINING AND SPEAKING ENGAGEMENTS

To contact Dr. Wolfelt about speaking engagements or training opportunities at his Center for Loss and Life Transition, email him at DrWolfelt@centerforloss.com.

ALSO BY ALAN WOLFELT

The Wilderness of Grief

FINDING YOUR WAY

You are grieving the death of someone you love.

Think of your grief as a wilderness—a vast, mountainous forest. You are in the wilderness now. You are in the midst of unfamiliar and often brutal surroundings. You are cold and tired.

Yet you must journey through this wilderness. To find your way out, you must become acquainted with its terrain and learn to follow the sometimes hard-to-find path that leads to healing.

This excerpted version of Understanding Your Grief is approachable and appropriate for all mourners, making it an ideal book for the bedside or coffee table. Pick it up before bed and read just a few pages. You'll be carried off to sleep by its gentle, affirming messages of hope and healing.

ISBN 978-1-879651-52-4 • 112 pages • hardcover • $15.95

All Dr. Wolfelt's publications can be ordered by mail from:
Companion Press | 3735 Broken Bow Road, Fort Collins, Colorado 80526
Phone: (970) 226-6050 | www.centerforloss.com

The Depression of Grief

COPING WITH YOUR SADNESS AND KNOWING WHEN TO GET HELP

When someone you love dies, it's normal and necessary to grieve. Grief is the thoughts and feelings you have inside you, and sadness is often the most prominent and painful emotion. In other words, it's normal to be depressed after a loss. This compassionate guide will help you understand your natural depression, express it in ways that will help you heal, and know when you may be experiencing a more severe or clinical depression that would be eased by professional treatment. A section for caregivers that explores the new DSM-5 criteria for Major Depression is also included.

ISBN 978-1-61722-193-4 • 128 pages • softcover • $14.95

Healing Your Grieving Heart

100 PRACTICAL IDEAS

When someone loved dies, we must express our grief if we are to heal. In other words, we must mourn. But knowing what to do with your grief and how to mourn doesn't always come naturally in our mourning-avoiding culture.

This book offers 100 practical ideas to help you practice self-compassion. Some of the ideas teach you the principles of grief and mourning. The remainder offer practical, action-oriented tips for embracing your grief. Each also suggests a carpe diem, which will help you seize the day by helping you move toward healing today.

ISBN 978-1-879651-25-8 • 128 pages • softcover • $11.95